Meet the A-Lee Kids

Book 1

by Wayne James Coleman

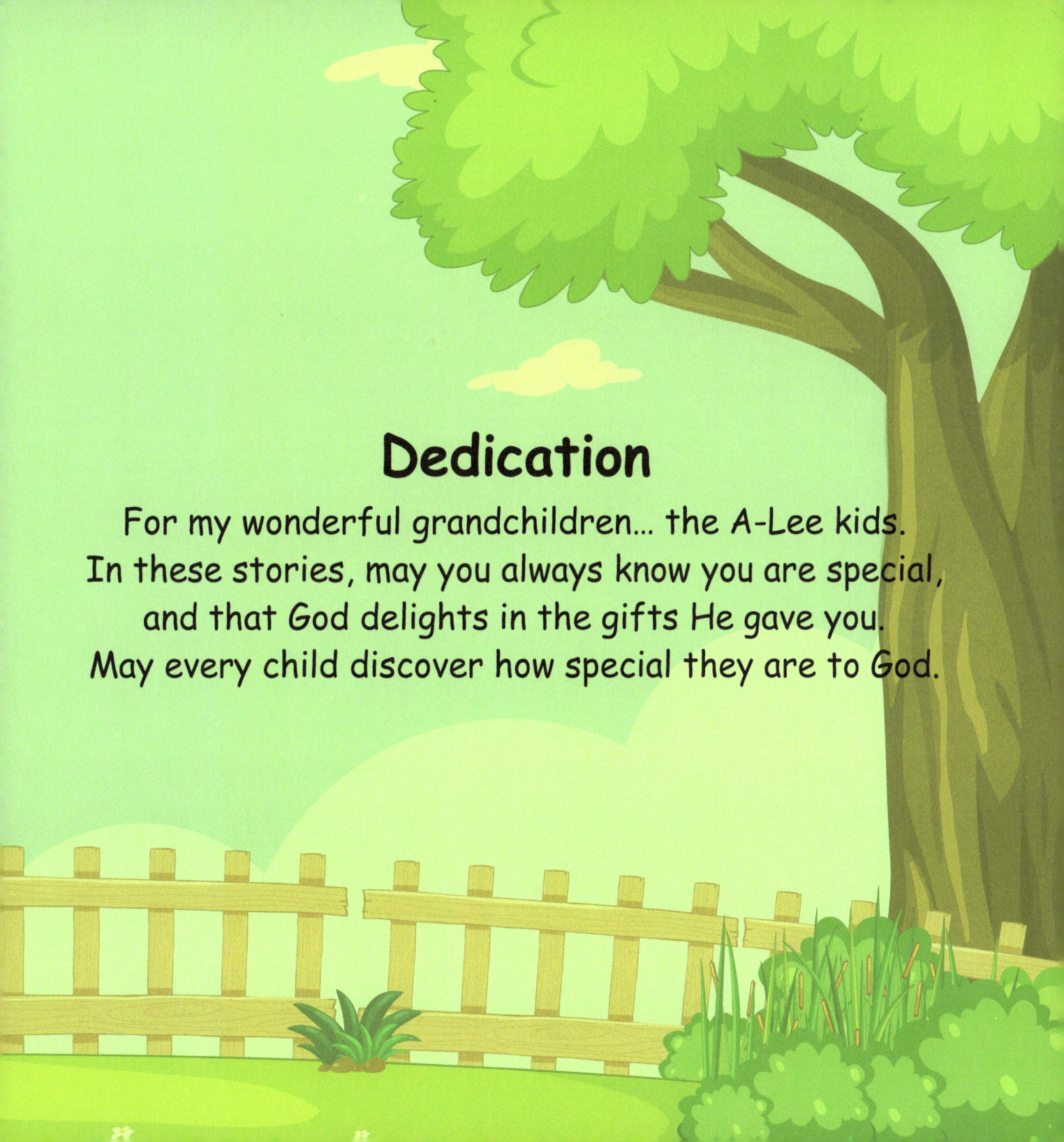

Dedication

For my wonderful grandchildren... the A-Lee kids.
In these stories, may you always know you are special,
and that God delights in the gifts He gave you.
May every child discover how special they are to God.

Acknowledgement

To my grandchildren — Josh, Ava, Chase, and Madalyn — whose childhood wonder first inspired the A-Lee Kids stories. Though you've grown, these stories remain a celebration of those joyful years we shared.

To my sister, Sharon Bower, who sees more in me than I ever see in myself.

And to my wife, Deborah, who always points me in the right direction.

This is Joshua A-Lee, but everyone calls him Josh. Josh is twelve. He is the oldest of the A-Lee Kids. Josh is the Thinker.

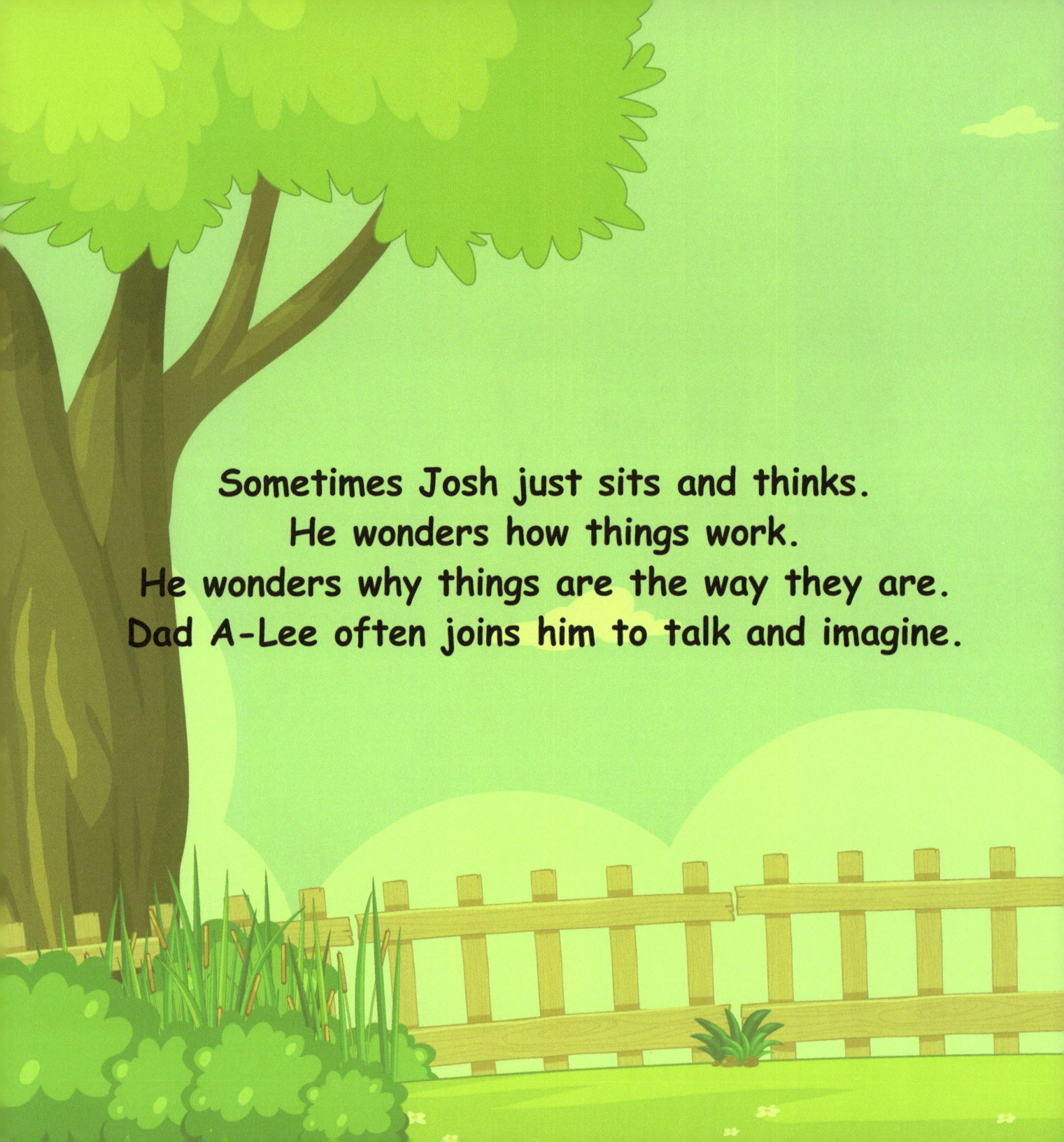

Sometimes Josh just sits and thinks.
He wonders how things work.
He wonders why things are the way they are.
Dad A-Lee often joins him to talk and imagine.

In the backyard, Mom A-Lee has a garden.
Josh watches her plant tiny seeds.
Mom shows Josh how to water and weed and gently pulls weeds.

One day, tiny green stems popped up!

Another day, Mom A-Lee pulls out weeds.
"Why do you do that?" asked Josh.
"So the baby plants can grow strong," says Mom.
"Watch carefully," says Dad.

Then Josh sees a little orange head peeking out of the ground. "What's that?" he asks.

"Wait," says Mom.
"Not yet. You'll see something amazing," says Dad.

One day, Mom lets Josh pull the green top.
Up comes a big, crunchy C_R__O_T.
Can you guess?

This is Ava A-Lee. Ava is eight.
She is the second A-Lee Kid.
She loves to read.

Sometimes Ava reads so much that she forgets to eat lunch.
She reads at the table.

She reads in bed.
She even reads in the car, where bumps make the words wiggle.

Books take her on adventures.
She climbs mountains.
She rides rocket ships.
She loves poems most of all.

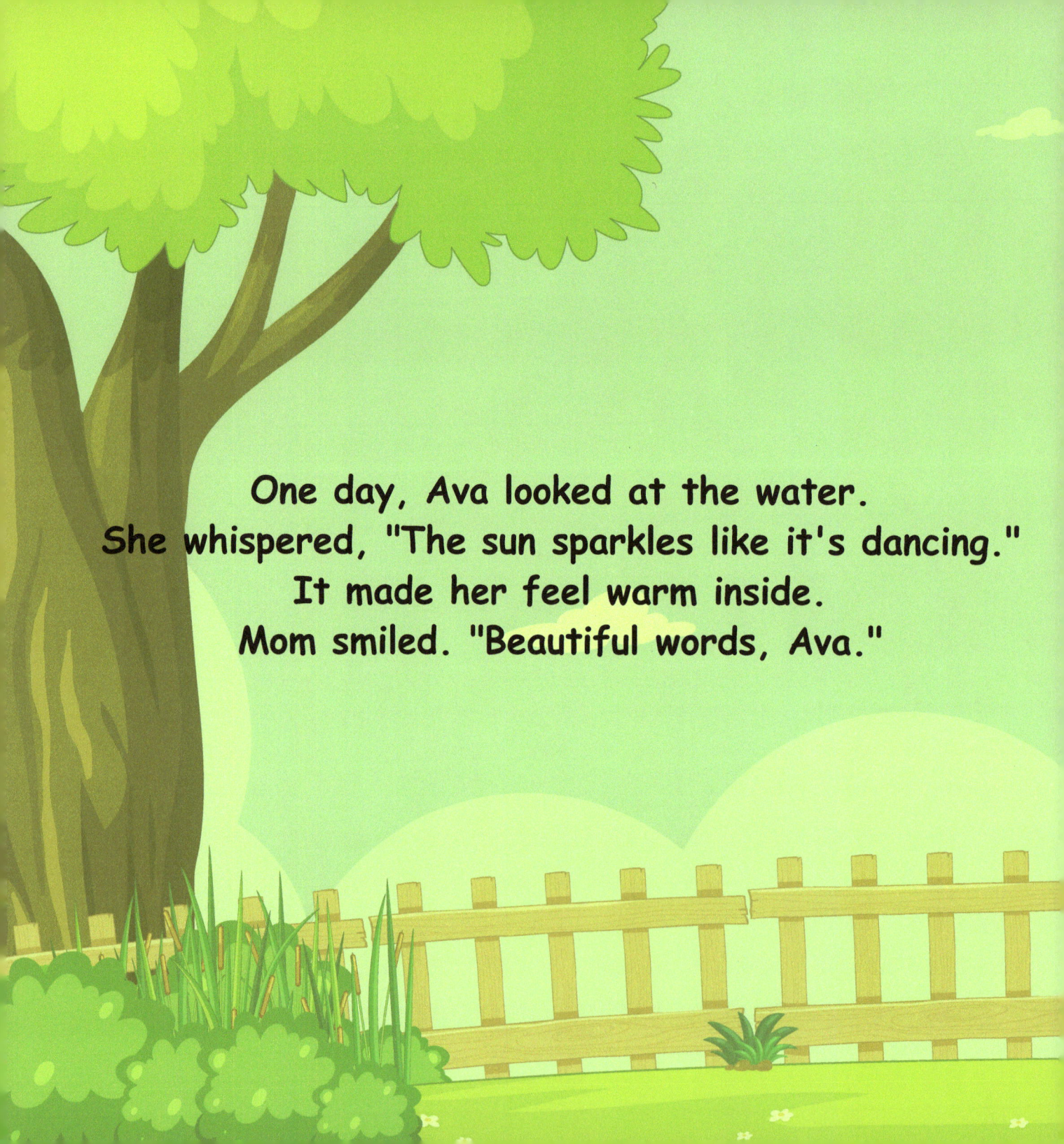

One day, Ava looked at the water.
She whispered, "The sun sparkles like it's dancing."
It made her feel warm inside.
Mom smiled. "Beautiful words, Ava."

Her brothers and cousin didn't like poems as much. But Ava didn't mind.

This is Chase A-Lee.
Chase is six. He is the third A-Lee Kid.
Everyone calls him the Explorer.

Chase crawls on the ground to see bugs.
He fills his pockets with rocks, feathers, and sometimes worms!
Dad laughs and whispers, "Keep exploring, Chase."

One day, Chase finds a caterpillar.
It wiggles. It crawls. It climbs a branch.

Then it wraps itself up tight.
"It's the caterpillar's house!" Chase shouted.

He goes to get Josh.
Josh says, "Something amazing will happen soon."

From his window, Chase watched and watched.

Then one day—something moves!
Out came a butterfly.
A beautiful butterfly.

"Wow," said Chase.
"How did it do that?"
Chase loved exploring, even if no one else did.

This is Madalyn A-Lee.
Madalyn is four.
She loves to dance.

She twirls in the kitchen.
She spins in the yard.

She dances through the living room. Sometimes she spins so much that she falls down laughing.

Whenever she feels sad, she just dances.
She thinks dancing makes the world happier.
Ava and Chase cheer her on.

One day, Madalyn asked,
"Why don't you like dancing like I do?"

Chase said, "I like exploring."
Ava said, "I like reading."
So they went to see Josh.
Dad and Mom smiled as they watched.

Josh was sitting under a tree, thinking.
"Why are we all so different?" they asked.
Josh smiled. "I can explain."

"Look at Mom's garden. Each plant is different."

"Each story Ava reads is different. Each bug Chase finds is different."

"Each dance you spin, Madalyn, is different too.
God made each of us special.
And it's okay to be different."

One sunny day, Madalyn's parents came too.
They brought a basket full of food, and everyone
had a picnic in the garden.
Different families, one big happy family.
God made each of us special—and loved.

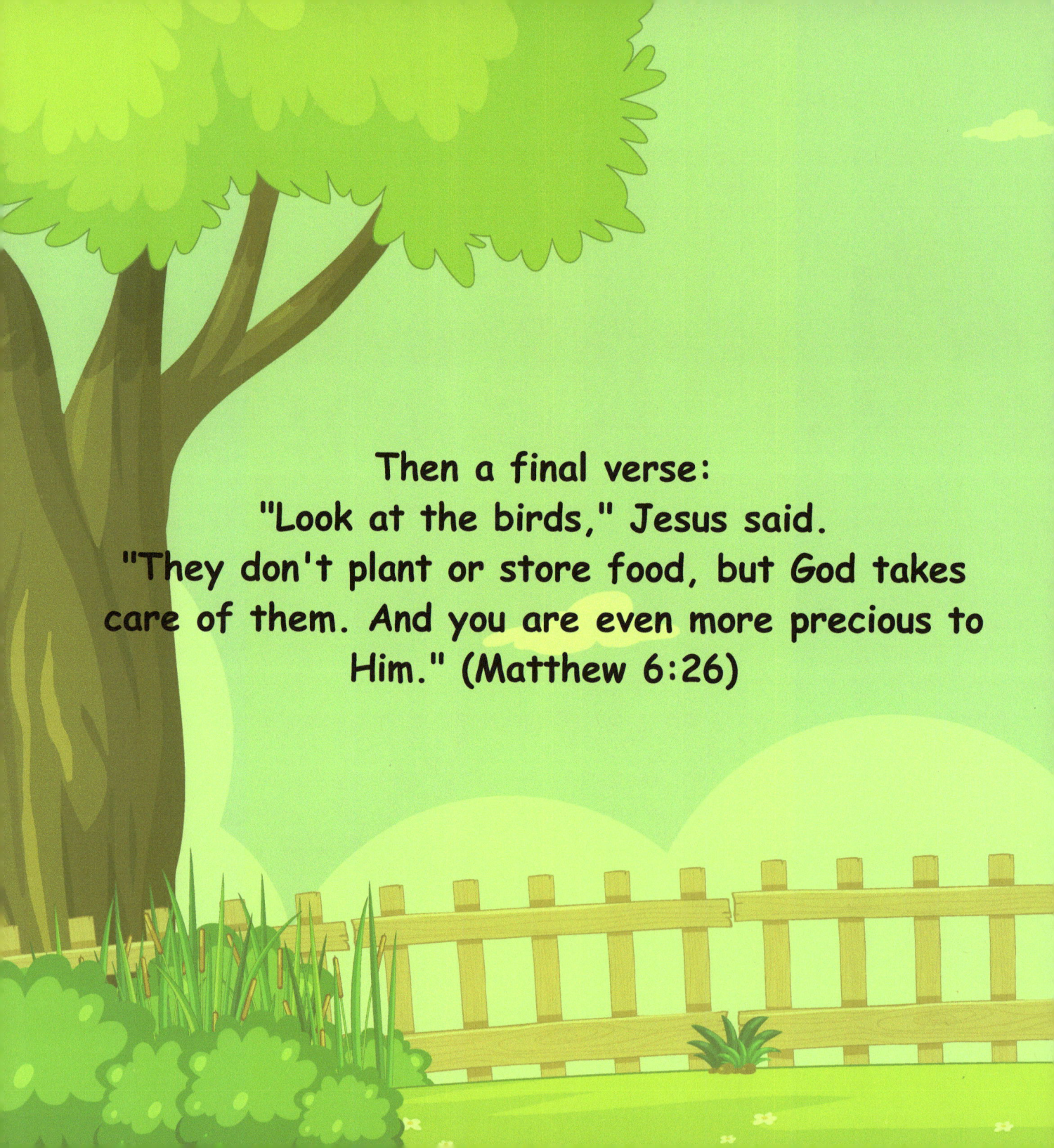

Then a final verse:
"Look at the birds," Jesus said.
"They don't plant or store food, but God takes care of them. And you are even more precious to Him." (Matthew 6:26)

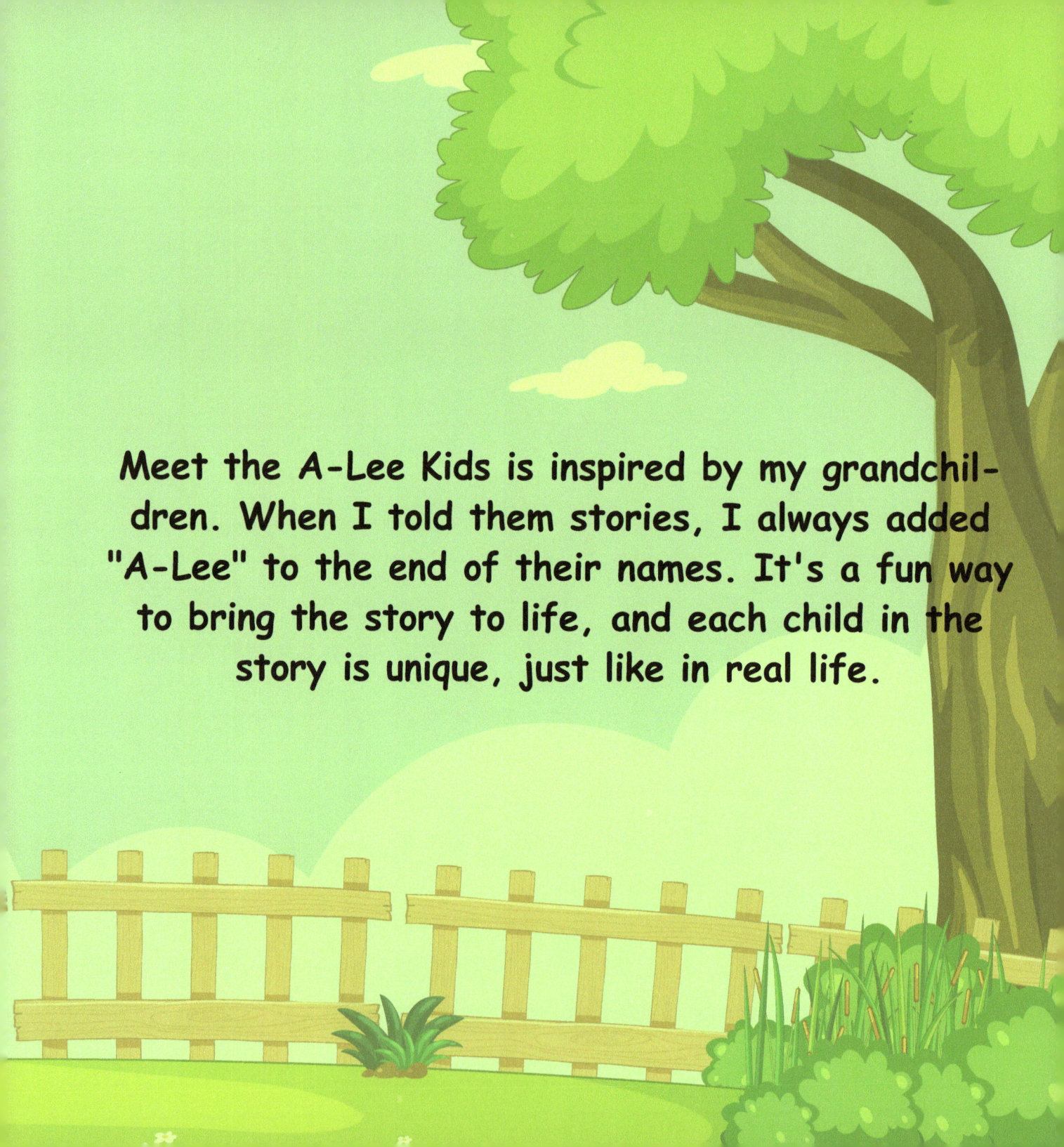

Meet the A-Lee Kids is inspired by my grandchildren. When I told them stories, I always added "A-Lee" to the end of their names. It's a fun way to bring the story to life, and each child in the story is unique, just like in real life.

www.ingramcontent.com/pod-product-compliance
Lightning Source LLC
Chambersburg PA
CBHW041113070526
44584CB00002B/150